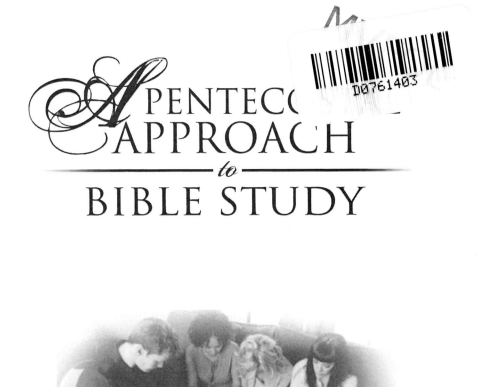

A PENTEC[OSTAL] APPROACH *to* BIBLE STUDY

William A. Simmons, Ph.D.

Enliven Path to Discipleship
Bible Study Series

TABLE OF CONTENTS

Foreword..iv

Introduction 9

Understanding Inductive Bible Study................................. 15

Discover God's Word for Yourself 17

Discern the Meaning of the Text... 23

Devote Oneself to God and His Calling............................. 29

Disciple Oneself and Others in the Word 33

Tens Tips for Starting an Inductive Bible Study
in a Local Church or Small Group................................. 37

A Working Example of an Inductive Bible Study.............. 43

Discover: Helping Questions 47

Discern: Helping Tools (Sample Helping Tools and Key) 51

The Text with Helping Tools Applied............................ 54

The Interpretation 59

Devote: Questions that Encourage Discipleship 63

Disciple: A Call to Commitment................................... 67

A Suggested Schedule for a Twelve-Week IBS Program 71

Concluding Thoughts 85

FOREWORD

Congratulations! You have just made a strategic leadership decision for those whom the Lord has placed in your care. By electing to learn what Inductive Bible Study is and how to lead others in this exciting and effective method of studying God's Word, you have charted a path of discipleship for your people. Not only will they become more familiar with the content of the Bible, but they will be challenged to make God's Word real in their lives. Moreover, as a result of this special ministry, your people will learn how to do Inductive Bible Study on their own. So as leader, if you do your job well, the skills that you learn as a result of working through this *Guide* will become their skills too. Thus by learning and teaching Inductive Bible Study, you will in fact be making "disciples of all nations" (Matt 28:19).

In short, this *Guide* is a tool for ministry. God can use it to change lives for Christ, and by extension, make an impact upon the whole church. Keep this vision in mind as you prayerfully work through this manual. Realize that learning, teaching and promoting Inductive Bible Study is a divine appointment for you and your church. With God's help and by the power of the Holy Spirit, your efforts as leader will positively impact the Kingdom of God for years to come.

It is my prayer that this study initiative in God's Word serves as a turning point for you and your church.

May God richly bless you as you minister God's truth to others!

William A. Simmons, Ph.D.

BIBLE STUDY

INTRODUCTION

A Pentecostal Approach to Bible Study

Introduction

Therefore go and make disciples of all nations, baptizing them in the name of the Father and of the Son and of the Holy Spirit, and teaching them to obey everything I have commanded you. And surely I am with you always, to the very end of the age (Matt. 28:19-20).

These are the last words of Jesus in the Gospel of Matthew. They are commonly known as the "Great Commission" because they clearly set forth God's will for the Church. We are to go forth and make disciples, baptize new converts, and teach all things that Jesus commanded. It is no accident that the charge to "make disciples" is closely linked with the ministry of "teaching." That is, the primary way that disciples are made is by truly learning and doing the Word of God. When one considers that the Greek word for "disciple" (*mathētēs*) literally means "a learner" and that the word for "teach" (*didaskō*) means "to point with the finger," the connection between Christian growth and biblical instruction is clear.

"Making disciples" in the early church did not just involve learning what Jesus said. Rather, becoming a disciple meant putting His words and deeds into practice. So discipleship is really about spiritual formation and growth.

For this reason, the real purpose of Inductive Bible Study (IBS) is not simply the memorization of Scripture. Rather, IBS is dedicated to the authentic spiritual development of the believer. Its goal is that *through the Word*, the believer might be empowered to reach a new level of spiritual maturity (Eph. 4:15). That is, as the student gets into God's Word, or more importantly, as God's Word gets into the student, they will increasingly be transformed into the image of Christ (Rom. 12:1-2).

It is only through God's help and the empowering of the Holy Spirit that the promise of IBS can come to fruition. That is why this present study is more like a spiritual journey than just a Bible study. The student is launched upon a *Path to Discipleship*; one born along by the Spirit at every turn.

All of this means that there must be a strong devotional element to IBS. Indeed, at strategic points along the way, the student will be invited to *Pause for Prayer*. Here they will experience a time of devotion that is intended to prepare them for the next important step of their journey. Often this next step will be a *call to action*. Again, for IBS, it is not enough to simply know God's Word, but one must also do God's Word. So in addition to the devotional aspect of IBS, there will also be a clear emphasis on sanctification or holiness. IBS is about changing believers' lives for the better! So with the help of God, the student will be challenged to make a personal covenant with the Bible.

This is where another important part of IBS comes in—*journaling*. Keeping a spiritual log of what we have experienced through God's Word, and what we have personally committed to in God's Word, is an essential aspect of IBS. One would not go on a trip of a lifetime without recording the highlights of that experience. The purpose of keeping such a journal or logbook is so that you can recall, and to some extent, relive what you experienced at that important time in your life. The same holds true for one's life-changing journey in IBS. You will want to record what the Spirit is saying to you as you commit to actualizing God's Word in your life. In this way you will be able to chart your spiritual progress along the way. Also the very act of writing down your *personal covenant* with the Word will help you follow through on your promises to God.

Herein lies the purpose of this *Guide*. It is to empower the Church to make disciples by effectively teaching God's Word. This goal will be accomplished by way of the Inductive Bible Study method. By working through this *Guide*, one will soon discover that Inductive Bible Study (IBS) is an enjoyable yet highly successful method of learning the Bible.

In pursuit of this goal, this *Guide* will . . .

1. Set forth and explain the basic principles of Inductive Bible Study (IBS)

2. Provide the group leader with the necessary tools to do an inductive study on any book of the Bible

3. Include an instructional sample of an inductive study on Mark 2:1-12

4. Supply a suggested weekly schedule for a twelve-week IBS program.

The law of the Lord is perfect,

refreshing the soul.

The statutes of the Lord are trustworthy,

making wise the simple.

The precepts of the Lord are right,

giving joy to the heart.

The commands of the Lord are radiant,

giving light to the eyes.

The fear of the Lord is pure,

enduring forever.

The decrees of the Lord are firm,

and all of them are righteous.

They are more precious than gold,

than much pure gold;

they are sweeter than honey,

than honey from the honeycomb.

Psalms 19:7-10

BIBLE STUDY

Understanding
Inductive Bible Study

Understanding
Inductive Bible Study

The basic principles of IBS are easy to understand and its methods are effective. That is why IBS has proven to be so powerful for discipleship. It only follows that a working knowledge of IBS will certainly enhance ministerial effectiveness in the local church. Herein lies the goal of this section. By grasping the main points of IBS and by following the step-by-step example of how IBS works, the discipleship potential of the church will be greatly increased.

The following orientation and practice will be structured around the four principal steps of the IBS method. These steps are: 🔍 **Discover** ... 🕯️ **Discern** ... ✝ **Devote** ... 🐟 **Disciple.** You will notice that each step has a particular symbol attached to it. These symbols (and others) will be repeated throughout the study. In this way IBS builds in elements of continuity and recognition for the student.

Each step naturally follows on from the one before it, and all the steps work together to accomplish the all-important goal of IBS: a deeper understanding of God's Holy Word.

So let's get started!

PENTECOSTAL APPROACH
to
BIBLE STUDY

DISCOVER
God's Word *for* Yourself

DISCOVER
God's Word *for* Yourself

This caption goes a long way in answering the question: "What is Inductive Bible Study"? IBS is simply discovering God's Word for yourself. It is reading God's Word with a purpose. So IBS is an active, hands-on approach to the Bible that presents the Scriptures in an immediate and personal way. In short, IBS is a method of studying the Bible by which the reader is "drawn into" the words of Scripture. Indeed, the literal meaning of the word *inductive* is "to be drawn into" or "to be led into." So IBS is the process by which the believer is directly and personally "drawn into" the Word of God. By way of this direct and total immersion in the Bible, the reader is "led into" a deeper and much more satisfying understanding of God and the Gospel. This means that IBS does not simply teach "prepackaged" doctrinal statements from days gone by. Rather, it empowers the sincere student of Scripture to "*dis*-cover" divine truth in the here and now. In fact, IBS reflects the ancient Greek word for truth (*alēthea*) which literally means "to *un*-cover." This means that IBS enables the student to "*un*-cover" or to "*dis*-cover" the truth of God contained in His Word. Most importantly, IBS "makes room" for the Holy Spirit "to lead us" (or "induct" us!) into all truth (John 16:13). In this way, the prayerful believer is "drawn into" the Word by the Spirit and begins an exciting journey of discovery—a journey that reveals God's wisdom every step of the way.

In summary, IBS supplies the student with a fun, repeatable pattern of study that directly engages the Scriptures. This framework for study can be applied to the whole Word of God, from Genesis to Revelation. So this enjoyable method of study can be used every time a believer picks up the Bible.

This first step in the study, **Discover**, simply involves a careful reading of the text. It is here that the student allows himself or herself to be completely drawn into the words of the Bible. Resisting the temptation to leap ahead and ask, "What does this passage *mean*?" during the **Discover** step of study, the student should repeatedly ask the question, "What does the Scripture *say*?" So the active learning principle here is *observation*, not interpretation. The IBS method will certainly include interpretation, but that will come later. For now, the task at hand is to simply but intently *observe* what the Word says. This is not a passive exercise! Rather, the student must actively *identify* important features contained in the Word.

In order to enhance the student's powers of observation, the **Discover** step involves the following activities:

1. Carefully read the text, then . . . read it again!

2. Rigorously bring the "five W's and one H" questions to bear upon the selected text: Who? What? When? Where? Why? and How? These questions may also be called "Helping Questions" because they help the believer grasp the words and elements that are central to the text at hand. For example, if the Scriptures say, "At that time Jesus went through the grainfields on the Sabbath" (Matt. 12:1), the first Helping Question might be, *"When did this happen?"* The next step is to write down the answer to this question. Another question that might be brought to bear on the text is, *"Where did this happen?"* The answer to this question should be written down as well. This process of posing questions and writing out the answers should continue until the student is satisfied that he or she knows the content of the passage. One might feel that such questions are simple and the answers obvious. But it is the overall effect of the questions and answers that is important here. Just the activity of deciding what question should be asked of the text and then actually writing down the answer will help one master the content of the Scriptures.

It should be noted, too, that in some cases, not all of these questions will work for the passage selected. For example, the Helping Question *"How?"* may not make any sense for the Scriptures under consideration. If this is the case, then don't use that question. Also, these questions do not have to be used in any particular order. Any question that helps one get in touch with the content of the passage is a good question. This is a strong point of the IBS method. The student is able to adapt aspects of the method to meet the concerns that he or she has at that time. There is no right order, and there are no wrong answers. The point is to keep engaging the text in a determined way.

Here are some possible Helping Questions that may assist in learning God's Word:

1. *What* is the context of the passage? This question helps to identify what comes before and what comes after the Scriptures being studied.

2. *When* (chronologically) did this great event happen?

3. *Where* (geographically) did this story occur?

4. *Who* are the main characters mentioned in this passage?

5. *What* role does each person play in the story?

6. *When* did each part of the story occur?

7. *How* did God respond to the people?

8. *Why* was the gospel rejected in this instance?

9. *What* does this tell us about the hearts of the people?

10. *Why* were no miracles done here?

11. *How* does the Lord deal with those who oppose Him?

12. *What* should the people have said in this case?

There is no limit to the number and kinds of questions that can be addressed to the text. The important point is that each student should creatively find ways to dig into the Scriptures. In this way, individually crafted questions and answers will address the special concerns of the student who made them. So again, the number and nature of the questions are not important: it is the activity and process that are important here. Believers are now purposefully getting into the Word of God for themselves!

Now that the student has a firm grasp on the raw data of the text, so to speak, they are ready for the second important step of the IBS method: **Discern**.

PENTECOSTAL APPROACH
to
BIBLE STUDY

DISCERN
The Meaning *of the* TEXT

DISCERN
The Meaning *of the* TEXT

The **Discover** step allowed the student to *observe* the "lay of the land," so to speak. It permitted the student to acquire the fundamental "facts" contained in the text. The **Discern** step empowers the student to really "excavate" or "dig beneath" the surface of the passage so that they might understand its *meaning*. So the active learning principle here is *interpretation*. The importance of this facet of IBS cannot be overemphasized if it can be recalled that the word for "interpretation" in the Greek is *diermēneuō* (see 1 Cor. 12:30: 14:5, 13, 27) and literally means "to thoroughly unseal." It is from this Greek word that we get our English word *hermeneutics,* which is the art of interpretation. So in the **Discern** step of IBS, the student is "unsealing" the meaning of the text.

In many ways the **Discern** step is the most creative and fun part of the IBS method. And by design, it is the most productive as well. In this step, the student is to look for important words that convey central ideas found in the passage. Such words might include: Father, Son, Spirit, sin, repentance, forgiveness, healing, salvation, and the like. Also, the student is to be on the lookout for prominent features of the passage, such as repetition, rhyming, comparison, contrast . . . anything that might help reveal the meaning of the text.

Here comes the really fun part. The student is now ready to create a system of "Helping Tools" so that he or she might keep track of all of the special features and words found in the text. These Helping Tools might consist of color-coding key terms, circling repeated phrases, developing small symbols for important theological ideas . . . anything that will help them discern the meaning of the Word of God.

For example, the student might choose the color red to mark every occurrence relating to the blood of Jesus, or to the Atonement. The color blue might stand for royalty and mark any references to God the Father. The color green would point to creation and brown would reference any geographic location. An AΩ would refer to Christ, and a small dove symbol would reference the Holy Spirit. The infinity ∞ symbol would mean "heaven" or "eternal life" and a small house ⌂ could be the Temple or reflect the indwelling of

God. A small clock ⏱ could mark all references to time. In addition to all of these Helping Tools, one might use circles, brackets, and underlining to mark off important aspects of the text. Also, different colors of highlighting could be used to mark the text as well. Again, the number and kinds of Helping Tools are limitless. This means that each student's collection of Helping Tools will be different, and that is how it should be. There are only two important rules that apply here:

1. The student should thoughtfully choose a marking system that makes sense to them. That is, they should choose colors and symbols that, in their way of thinking, convey ideas and principles found in the Scriptures.

2. The student should be consistent in his/her use of the Helping Tools they have created. If red refers to the blood of Christ in Romans, then words marked in red in the Epistle to the Hebrews should also mean the blood of Christ.

In short order, these Helping Tools will become second nature for the student. They will employ these signs, symbols, and marks every time they have a passage of Scripture before them. The days of simply *reading* the text will be over! From now on, they only *study* God's Word.

Moreover, when they do study the Bible, they will study it inductively.

Now, literally, comes the moment of truth. The student has arrived at the point of *interpretation*. They can now step back and take stock of all of the data that has been "un-covered" through the use of the Helping Questions employed in the **Discover** step. Then all of this information can now be integrated into all of the patterns, repetitions and concepts that have surfaced through the use of the Helping Tools. Indeed, the student has arrived at the place where they can responsibly ask questions like these:

- "What is God saying in this passage of Scripture?"

- "How might the meaning of God's Word in this passage relate to other portions of the Bible?"

- "What do these Scriptures mean to the church in general?"

- "What do these Scriptures mean to me personally?"

- "What does God want me to do with this new-found knowledge of His Word?"

Again, since the student has disciplined himself or herself to go through the IBS process, they are now in a position to give informed answers to questions like those listed above. For example, if the passage contains a number of dove ⚊ symbols, then the person and work of the Holy Spirit is in view. If blue for the Father is contrasted with the repeated mention of sin, then the holiness of God and the need for forgiveness comes through. And finally, if red for the Atonement is central to the story then the meaning of the passage becomes clear: God is holy and sinners are in need of divine forgiveness. This forgiveness is secured through the blood of Christ and made real in our lives by the person and work of the Spirit.

At the end of this *Guide*, a working example of an IBS lesson will be presented. This lesson will demonstrate the four major steps of the IBS method. All of the Helping Questions and an array of Helping Tools will be brought to bear upon a specific passage of Scripture. In this way, one will be able to see all of the critical aspects of the IBS method at work.

PENTECOSTAL
APPROACH *to*
BIBLE STUDY

DEVOTE
Oneself to God *and*
His Calling

Devote
Oneself to God *and*
His Calling

The student may now proceed to the next, and certainly, the most important part of the IBS process. Indeed, there must be a strong devotional element in IBS if it is to accomplish its true goal: to disciple believers in Christ. This means that in light of their new understanding of God and His Word, the student is now to be truly and completely "drawn into" the very voice of God calling forth from the text. This step can never simply be an academic exercise. On the contrary, because they have carefully worked through the Word, they are now prepared to receive "the Spirit of wisdom and revelation" as promised in Ephesians 1:17. It is here that the life-changing power of the living Word (Heb. 4:12) can have its way in the heart of every believer. It is here that the living presence of the Logos (John 1:1-14) makes Himself real to those fully devoted to God and His Kingdom.

The operative words here are *commitment* and *obedience*. While working through the **Devote** step of the study, the student is to sincerely open his/her heart to such questions as these:

- ◆ "What does God expect me to do in light of what I have learned?"

- ◆ "Is God calling me to a new aspect of ministry?"

- ◆ "Does God want to clarify some misperception I've had for a long time?"

- ◆ "Is God calling me to repentance through His Word?"

- ◆ "Is He wanting me to receive forgiveness or, perhaps more importantly, to give forgiveness?"

- ◆ "Does God want me to grow in faith and trust in Him?"

- ◆ "Is God calling me to a deeper level of commitment to Him?"

Clearly the **Devote** step of IBS is to be bathed in prayer. This is why the *Pause for Prayer* aspect of IBS is so important. It is the interpretive step that lends itself to authentic transformation by the Word through the empowerment of the Spirit. The **Devote** step is nothing less than the personal experience of Romans 12:1, which states, "Therefore, I urge you, brothers, in view of God's mercy, to offer your bodies as living sacrifices, holy and pleasing to God—this is your spiritual act of worship." Thus an authentic realization of the **Devote** step of IBS works toward that renewing of the mind (Rom. 12:2) so critical for sanctification or holiness (Rom. 6:1-14).

By nature, the **Devote** step is a deeply personal aspect of IBS. For this reason, the students should be encouraged to keep a spiritual journal, or logbook, as they work through the assignments. In this way they can record their personal reflections and commitments they have made to the Word. The very act of writing things down tends to strengthen one's resolve to follow through on one's personal covenant with the Lord. Also, over time, a pattern of spiritual growth will emerge. This kind of journal can serve as an invaluable personal reference in the years to come.

Now that the student has acquired a deeper understanding of the Word and also experienced a closer walk with God (Rom. 8:1-5), he or she can proceed to the **Disciple** step of the IBS method. It is here that the "salt and light" (Matt 5:13-14) aspects of IBS really come into play. As salt, the scripturally informed believer preserves God's truth in the world. As light, they illumine God's will and way to those in need of salvation.

BIBLE STUDY

DISCIPLE
Oneself *and* Others *in the* Word

DISCIPLE
Oneself *and* Others *in the* Word

The **Disciple** step is a *call to action*! That is why the operative words for the **Disciple** step are *obedience* and *commitment*. It is here that the student is expected to take real steps toward spiritual change. This is the aspect of IBS where true spiritual formation can occur. With God's help and through the power of the Holy Spirit, the student will have an opportunity to make a personal covenant with the mandates set forth in the Bible.

As far as the IBS method is concerned, the **Disciple** step will look something like this:

In light of the spiritual lessons that I have learned in this study, I make a personal covenant with God's Word to . . .

◆ Tear down any barriers that might keep me from drawing closer to God

◆ Willingly receive God's personal will for my life, even if it is very different from what I expected

◆ Act without hesitation to the healing voice of Jesus in my life.

Yet it is important to note that IBS is not just about the individual. It is about fulfilling the Great Commission to go out into all the world *and make disciples*. So the mission of IBS is not complete until it not only disciples the individual student, but it also motivates that student to go out and disciple others in the Lord. In an actual IBS lesson, this aspect of discipleship might look like this:

> The spiritual growth that you have experienced as a result of this study is not meant to be kept to yourself. You are not only to be discipled in the Word, but you are to go out and disciple others through the Word. Perhaps there is someone in your circle of influence that needs to draw closer to Jesus so that they can be healed, and fully experience His lordship again. Pray that the Lord will give you the wisdom and the strength to lead others along this pathway to discipleship.

Show me your ways, Lord,

teach me your paths.

Guide me in your truth and teach me,

for you are God my Savior,

and my hope is in you all day long.

Psalms 25:4-5

A PENTECOSTAL APPROACH *to* BIBLE STUDY

TEN TIPS

for **Starting** *an*
Inductive Bible Study
in a
Local Church *or* **Small Group**

TEN TIPS

for **Starting** *an*
Inductive Bible Study
in a
Local Church *or* Small Group

Clearly, IBS is a powerful tool for discipleship. What follows are some practical guidelines for establishing IBS as an integral part of the local church and for leading a small group:

1. *Communication and planning are essential for the success of any IBS program.* First, any introduction of IBS to a church or group must be announced in advance. A brief explanation of what IBS is and how it works can be given at this time. Lastly, a specific date must be set for the first session, and some indication of the length and goals of the program should be stated.

2. *The leader of an IBS session must have clear goals in mind.* The length of the study series (6, 10, or 12 weeks) should be carefully determined and explained. It might be good to use one week to go over the **Discover . . . Discern . . .**

Devote . . . Disciple steps contained in this *Guide*. The leader must be intentional about what section of Scripture or book of the Bible will be studied. This would be a good time to share what kinds of spiritual lessons will be learned if one completes the study. Then all aspects of IBS are tailored to reach these goals.

3. *Encourage each student to make a covenant with the Word.* For example, if the IBS group meets on a Wednesday night, then each student should commit to doing about three hours of "homework" throughout the week. Then they should be prepared to share their findings and insights in a group setting the following Wednesday night. This pattern will continue until the IBS series is completed. A final week can be devoted to a "wrap up" session. At this time students will be given an opportunity to share what IBS has meant to them. Also, a summary of the main points of the IBS can be reviewed at this time. Then the group can decide what study they will take up next.

4. *Express confidence in your students.* Your students should know from the start that IBS is a simple and enjoyable way to experience God's Word. Assure them that they can learn IBS and that it will soon become a regular part of their study of the Scriptures.

5. *The leader doesn't have to have all the answers.* In fact, the real goal of IBS is that the students should discover God's truth for themselves. So the leader of an IBS functions as an informed facilitator—one who

questions the students concerning *what the Bible says.* In most cases, the leader poses open-ended questions so that the students engage the Scriptures at a deeper level.

6. *Keep the students on the path of discovery.* A vital part of any IBS program is meeting in community for the purpose of discussing the lessons that have been assigned. This is an important part of the interpretive process. So each student should be given an opportunity to share their new understanding of the passage with the rest of the group. In this way each student can glean from his or her neighbor's understanding of the Word. This is also part of the interpretive process. By mutual sharing in community, a person is given the opportunity to embrace new ways of seeing God's Word.

7. *Keep the discussion going.* If a student is made to feel that he or she has "got it all wrong," or if in some way they are publicly embarrassed, the give-and-take dynamic of IBS will come to an end.

8. *Be prepared to give more.* Once the students have shared all that they have discovered about a particular passage, the group leader should be ready to supply any core insight that may have been overlooked by the group. That is to say, the group leader needs to study as much or even more than the students that make up the IBS group.

9. *The leader should begin each session with a quick summary of the main points that have been discovered to this point.* This helps all of the group members to "get on the same page" and also introduces the next lesson.

10. *Emphasize the pastoral aspect of IBS.* As leader, you are calling your students to authentically engage God's Word and to seek real change in their lives. Nothing could be more pastoral than that, and as teacher, you need to be prepared to shepherd your flock of students.

At any point in the IBS process, the group leader may want to round out strategic points in the study with a lecture-type presentation. The use of commentaries, Bible dictionaries, maps, timelines, and so forth, can greatly enhance the truths that the class has discovered by way of the inductive method.

You, however, must teach

what is appropriate to sound doctrine.

Titus 2:1

A PENTECOSTAL APPROACH *to* BIBLE STUDY

A Working Example of an Inductive Bible Study

A Working Example of an Inductive Bible Study

What follows is a sample IBS on Mark 2:1-12. The goal here is to provide a working example of each of the four major steps of the IBS method (**Discover . . . Discern . . . Devote . . . Disciple**). Procedurally, an unmarked copy of Mark 2:1-12 will be presented first. You will note that plenty of space has been left between the verses so that the various Helping Tools can be inserted directly into the text. This practice of leaving adequate space for marking the text will be used in each lesson of the *Discovery Guides (the Enliven Path to Discipleship Bible study series)*. Then the **Discover** step will be applied by posing a number of *Helping Questions* to this text. Following this, a number of *Helping Tools* will be developed to complete the **Discern** step of IBS. Then the **Devote** step will highlight the personal spiritual challenges contained in the text. Finally, the **Disciple** step will present the student with a call to action. Here the student will be challenged to make real change in their lives—the kind of change that is required by the Word of God.

THE TEXT

MARK 2:1-12

¹A few days later, when Jesus again entered Capernaum, the

people heard that he had come home. ² So many gathered

that there was no room left, not even outside the door, and

he preached the word to them. ³ Some men came, bringing to

him a paralytic, carried by four of them. ⁴ Since they could

not get him to Jesus because of the crowd, they made an

opening in the roof above Jesus and, after digging through

it, lowered the mat the paralyzed man was lying on. ⁵ When

Jesus saw their faith, he said to the paralytic, "Son, your sins

are forgiven." ⁶ Now some teachers of the law were sitting

there, thinking to themselves, [7] "Why does this fellow talk

like that? He's blaspheming! Who can forgive sins but God

alone?" [8] Immediately Jesus knew in his spirit that this was

what they were thinking in their hearts, and he said to them,

"Why are you thinking these things? [9] Which is easier: to

say to the paralytic, 'Your sins are forgiven,' or to say, 'Get

up, take your mat and walk'? [10] But that you may know that

the Son of Man has authority on earth to forgive sins . . ."

He said to the paralytic, [11] "I tell you, get up, take your mat

and go home." [12] He got up, took his mat and walked out in

full view of them all. This amazed everyone and they praised

God, saying, "We have never seen anything like this!"

PENTECOSTAL APPROACH *to* BIBLE STUDY

DISCOVER
God's Word *for* Yourself

DISCOVER
God's Word *for* Yourself

As has been already noted, in this step of IBS the student is to create a number of Helping Questions to "pry out" the facts contained in the selected text.

Helping Questions (The five W's and one H: Who? What? When? Where? Why? and How?)

Question: What is the context of the passage?

Answer: Before Mark 2:1, Jesus is conducting a charismatic ministry throughout the region of Galilee (1:39). He is healing lepers and casting out demons (1:39-42). After Mark 2:12, Jesus calls Levi—that is, Matthew the tax collector—to be His disciple (2:14). Jesus dines in Matthew's house and is criticized by the scribes and Pharisees for eating with tax collectors and sinners (2:15-16).

Question: How did Jesus' ministry affect the people?

Answer: He became so popular that He couldn't minister

in populated areas. He had to stay in remote
regions, but the people still found him (1:45).

Question: Where is Jesus at the opening of Mark 2?

Answer: He is preaching in a private home in Capernaum,
a city on the shore of the Sea of Galilee. People
throng to hear Him and even crowd the doorway
so that no more people can come in (2:2).

Question: Who are the main characters of the story?

Answer: Jesus, a paralyzed man, his four friends, the
scribes, and the people listening to Jesus preach

Question: What is the main action scene of the whole story?

Answer: Since the four men couldn't get in by the door,
they hoisted their paralyzed friend upon the
roof. They then hacked a hole in it, and lowered
him down in front of Jesus.

Question: How did Jesus respond to the paralyzed man?

Answer: One would expect that Jesus would heal him, but
He didn't—not at first.

Question: Why didn't Jesus heal the man?

Answer: He said that the man's sins were forgiven.

Question: What did the scribes do now?

Answer: They said that Jesus blasphemed, because only God can forgive sins.

Question: How did Jesus respond to that?

Answer: He healed the man.

Question: What happened next?

Answer: The man stood up on his feet, picked up his mat, and walked out before everyone. All the people were completely amazed for they had never seen anything like it.

A PENTECOSTAL APPROACH *to* BIBLE STUDY

DISCERN
The Meaning *of the* TEXT

DISCERN
The Meaning *of the* TEXT

Recall that in this step of IBS, the student is to develop a marking system that will track important words, concepts, and phrases contained in the text. That is, they are to highlight anything that they feel is significant for the meaning of the passage being studied.

A Key to the Sample Helping Tools
Applied to the Text in This Guide

Highlighting, Circling, Underlining,

Colored Shapes, etc. (shown in black & white here)

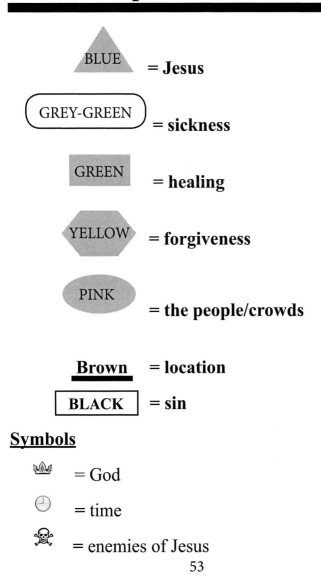

BLUE = Jesus

GREY-GREEN = sickness

GREEN = healing

YELLOW = forgiveness

PINK = the people/crowds

Brown = location

BLACK = sin

Symbols

= God

= time

= enemies of Jesus

53

THE TEXT
With Helping Tools Applied

MARK 2:1-12

¹A few days later 🕐, when Jesus again entered Capernaum,

the people heard that he had come home. ² So many gathered

that there was no room left, not even outside the door, and he

preached the word to them. ³ Some men came, bringing to him

a (paralytic,) carried by four of them. ⁴ Since they could not get

him to Jesus because of the crowd, they made an opening in the

roof above Jesus and, after digging through it, lowered the mat

the (paralyzed) man was lying on. ⁵ When Jesus saw their faith, he

said to the (paralytic,) "Son, your sins are forgiven." ⁶ Now some

teachers of the law were sitting there, thinking to themselves, [7] "Why does this fellow talk like that? He's blaspheming!

Who can forgive sins but 👑 God alone?" [8] Immediately Jesus

knew in his spirit that this was what 💀they were thinking in 💀

their hearts, and he said to 💀them, "Why are 💀you thinking

these things? [9] Which is easier: to say to the paralytic, 'Your

sins are forgiven,' or to say, 'Get up, take your mat and walk'? [10]

But that 💀you may know that the Son of Man has authority on

earth to forgive sins . . ." He said to the paralytic, [11] "I tell you,

get up, take your mat and go home." [12] He got up, took his mat

and walked out in full view of them all. This amazed everyone

and they praised 👑God, saying, "We have never seen anything

like this!"

Again, the reader is encouraged to take some time to carefully compare the unmarked text typed earlier in this *guide* with the marked text presented here. Now, using the key for the Helping Tools used in this lesson, trace out each color and symbol. As each color is traced out, the reader should make mental notes as to the meaning that begins to emerge from the study. For example, when you take note of all of the blue words, you will quickly **Discern** that Mark 2:1-12 has a lot to say about Jesus!

What follows will illumine even more truths that have arisen as a result of the IBS method.

Teach me your way, Lord,

that I may rely on your faithfulness;

give me an undivided heart,

that I may fear your name.

Psalms 86:11

BIBLE STUDY

DISCERN
The Interpretation

Discern

The Interpretation

The Helping Questions together with the Helping Tools have revealed much about the life and ministry of Jesus. Everything that precedes Mark 2:1-12, and the story that comes afterward, point to one central truth: Jesus is the promised Messiah of God—God's unique Son.

It is important for the student to take time when analyzing his or her marking system. They should trace out each color or highlighting individually, noting the particular significance of what emerges in each case. For example if a 👑 represents the kingdom of God and a cluster of crowns appear in the center of the passage, then the student should note that the kingdom of God forms the core of the story. Without carefully studying and taking notes on one's marking system, the value of the Helping Tools is lost.

For example, on this passage from Mark, the color coding reveals that the major players in this passage are Jesus and the crowds that press in on Him from all sides. The message here is that God has come *in Christ* and ministers to *His people.* The symbols and highlighting reveal that the paralytic and the scribes appear in the middle of the passage, as it were, holding together Jesus and the people. The paralytic, and, ironically, even Jesus' enemies affirm the divinity of Christ and His power to bring redemption and healing to those who are in need. They serve to prove that Jesus has the authority to forgive sins and heal, because He is God!

These are the big ideas that shine forth in this inductive study of Mark. Yet the IBS method has revealed more subtle, yet equally significant truths as well. This is true because there is much in this passage that addresses the believer "below the surface," so to speak. As will be seen, Mark 2:1-12 speaks to the heart and seeks to encourage genuine spiritual growth for everyone who truly desires a closer walk with God.

For example, according to the key, the color brown refers to physical location. As one traces this color throughout the marked text of Mark 2:1-12, one can see that the story starts out with a "wide-angle lens," so to speak. That is, the physical location is the entire city of Capernaum. But then the scene quickly narrows down to a house, and then to a crowded doorway. The scene tapers further still to an interior room of the house, and then penetrates to the thoughts of the heart. Finally, the view becomes that of a magnifying glass, zooming in for a close-up view of the human soul and the forgiveness of sins.

Another point that surfaces as a result of the Helping Tools is the placement of the actual healing in the story. Because of the dramatic beginning of the story (breaking a hole in the roof and lowering the paralytic through!), one would expect the healing to take place right off. Yet the color coding visually demonstrates that the healing actually happens at the end of the story. The message here is evident: as far as the kingdom of God is concerned, spiritual healing is top priority. Physical healing is good, but the forgiveness of sins is better.

Now that the sample **Discover** and **Discern** steps have been presented, it is time to move on to the **Devote** and **Disciple** steps of IBS.

$\mathcal{A}$ PENTECOSTAL $\mathcal{A}$PPROACH *to* BIBLE STUDY

DEVOTE
Oneself to God *and*
His Calling *in the* TEXT

Devote
Oneself to God *and*
His Calling *in the* Text

To this point, IBS has been dedicated to *getting the student into the Word*. However, the **Devote** step of IBS is dedicated to *getting the Word into the student*. It is here that the student purposefully embraces the spiritual lessons that have emerged throughout the study. Therefore, this is the step that calls for *real spiritual change* in the life of the student. This is true because as a result of all that they have learned through the IBS lesson, the students now recognize where they are in the Lord and also see where God wants them to be. Although prayer is a vital part in the **Discover** and **Discern** steps of IBS, arguably the **Devote** step should be infused with prayer from start to finish because this part of the study is where real spiritual formation can occur.

The **Devote** step is intensely personal by design. It is intended to bring the power of the Word to bear upon the human heart. It explicitly calls the student to make a personal covenant with the Word and to genuinely invite the work of the Spirit into his or her life. The very nature of the **Devote** step lends itself to journaling, or keeping a spiritual logbook. Recording one's commitment to change serves as a "promissory note" to God. Also, the journal serves as a written record for accountability, a record that can be referenced again and again as the student continues on the *Path to Discipleship.*

With regard to our sample lesson of Mark 2:1-12, the **Devote** step would consist of a number of commitments and questions that move the student in the direction of God's call in the text. The following offers some elements that might be included in the **Devote** section on this passage.

◆ With regard to the "Capernaum → house → heart →soul" pattern in Mark 2:1-12, to what extent have I allowed God to enter into my world, my house, my heart, and my soul?

◆ Like those who dug through the roof to get their friend near Jesus, am I ready to do anything, to break through any barriers, so that I might come into the presence of Jesus?

◆ Do I really value spiritual wholeness over physical healing?

Teach me, Lord, the way of your decrees,

that I may follow it to the end.

Psalms 119:33

A PENTECOSTAL APPROACH *to* BIBLE STUDY

DISCIPLE
Oneself *and* Others *in the* Word

DISCIPLE
Oneself *and* Others *in the* Word

If the **Devote** step is a call to spiritual commitment, the **Disciple** step is a call to concrete action. In this aspect of IBS, the student is to take definite steps to follow through on the spiritual commitments they have made in the **Devote** step. Here is where the student "incarnates" or makes the will of God become real in his or her own life. It is important for the student to be specific in this part of the study. They are not to speak in vague, general terms like, "I plan to be a better person." On the contrary, they should say something like, "*This week* I will spiritually encourage at least one person each and every day." With regard to Mark 2:1-12, the **Disciple** step might look something like this:

This week:

♦ I will invite Jesus into the "inner sanctuary" of my heart. I will do this by starting off each of my prayers by saying, "Lord Jesus, enter deeper into my heart than You have ever gone before."

♦ I will remove any barrier that impedes the intimate presence of the Lord in my life. I will do this by canceling some appointment or activity I had planned for this week, and in its place I will totally give myself to prayer.

◆ I will evaluate the content of my prayers and will determine to seek God's higher will in my life. That is, instead of seeking material prosperity or healing, I will seek forgiveness, the ability to humbly receive mercy, or ask God for a new spiritual gift so that I might minister more effectively.

Also as noted above, the **Disciple** step is not just about the individual, but is also about discipling others in the Lord. So in the case of our sample lesson, the student would pray for an opportunity to introduce others to the great spiritual truths contained in Mark 2:1-12. For those who are distant from the Lord, the student would emphasize the intimacy that Jesus desires to have in their lives. For those who have allowed carnal and worldly barriers to block the blessings of God, the student may suggest ways to dismantle these barriers so that the person might experience the full joy of the Lord again. For those whose vision is limited to the material things of this world, the student may be able to reveal the deep riches of God's grace. In short, the student is to actively seek opportunities to make discipes for Jesus.

Now that you, as leader, understand what IBS is and have become familiar with how it works, there is one big question that remains to be answered: "How can IBS be implemented in my local church or small group?" The following is a sample schedule for a twelve-week IBS program. This sample will give you practical tips on how to actually conduct such an inductive study. It should be added that these guidelines can be adapted for any length of an IBS program, whether it be six, ten, or twelve weeks in length.

A PENTECOSTAL APPROACH *to* BIBLE STUDY

A Suggested Schedule *for a* TWELVE-WEEK Inductive Bible Study Program

A Suggested Schedule for a
Twelve-Week Inductive Bible Study
Program

What follows is a step-by-step procedure for conducting a twelve-week IBS program on any book of the Bible. It is designed to give the group leader a framework for sequentially working through each study session found in the *Discovery Guides* of the *Enliven Path to Discipleship Bible study series*. In general, such a program would be divided as follows: During "Week One," the students will be taught the elementary principles of IBS contained in this *Guide* and be given an overview of what they can expect in the coming weeks. "Week Twelve" will be a wrap-up session wherein the main points of the study can be reviewed and summarized. The intervening ten weeks will consist of individual lessons printed in the *Discovery Guide*. This scheduling of sessions would work well for most of the books in the New Testament. If each lesson covered about one-half of a chapter, then in ten weeks one could study five chapters of the Bible. Except for Paul's letter to the Romans, 1 & 2 Corinthians, and the Epistle to the Hebrews, this twelve-week schedule would work well for the rest of the Epistles of the New Testament since these books contain no more than six chapters apiece.

A PENTECOSTAL APPROACH *to* BIBLE STUDY

WEEK ONE

How To Do An Inductive Bible Study

WEEK ONE

How to do an Inductive Bible Study

The major tasks for the group leader are these:

◆ To convey to the students that they are about to begin an exciting twelve-week (or ten or six-week) study program.

◆ Orient the students to the Inductive Bible Study method by sharing the principle points from this *Guide*.

This orientation should include:

1. Defining IBS

2. Teaching the four D's (**Discover . . . Discern . . . Devote . . . Disciple**) of the IBS method

3. Going over the working example of Mark 2:1-12 as set forth in this *Guide*

4. Giving a brief overview of the *Discovery Guide*

5. Announcing the assignment for Week Two.

This assignment will involve the student completing and studying Lesson One contained in the *Discovery Guide*. The student should be prepared to do thirty minutes of "homework" per night in the *Discovery Guide*. At the end of the week, when the whole study group meets together again, each student will have completed about three hours of study on a designated section. In this way, the student will be prepared to share his or her findings with the rest of the group. They will also be able to interact better with their fellow students and the group leader.

Make your face shine on your servant

and teach me your decrees.

Psalms 119:135

A PENTECOSTAL
APPROACH
to
BIBLE STUDY

WEEK TWO

*The Major Tasks
for the*
GROUP LEADER

Week Two

The following are six major tasks for the group leader:

1. Personally work through Lesson One of the *Discovery Guide*. This will not only give the group leader a thorough understanding of the lesson, but will also grant insight into what his or her students have been experiencing throughout the week.

2. Identify the essential learning points set forth in this lesson. This can be accomplished by repeatedly asking the question, "What should my students come away with in light of studying this lesson?"

3. Be prepared to give more than the students offer in class. That is, the group leader should be able to lead the students along the path to discipleship outlined in the *Discovery Guide* and also to offer additional insights on the text for that week. Also, the group leader should avail himself or herself of any supplemental helps, like commentaries, Bible dictionaries, timelines, and so forth, that might enhance the learning experience.

4. Lead an interesting and informative study session on the assigned lesson. Procedurally, the group leader can simply rehearse each step outlined in the *Discovery Guide* and open the class for a time of discussion and sharing. Also, the discussion group leader is to ask open-ended questions such as, "What do you think James means by . . . " or "What is the real issue being presented in this text?" Of course, each of these questions is designed to get the student to think about and understand the core teachings of James. The leader might want to jot down some of the responses made by the students. This will come in handy for the next step.

5. Continue to facilitate discussion on the **Discover** . . . **Discern** . . . **Devote** . . . **Disciple** steps of IBS by making frequent reference to the student responses that you have been listing on the board.

6. Assign Lesson 2 of the *Discovery Guide.*

For everything that was written in the past
was written to teach us, so that through the
endurance taught in the Scriptures
and the encouragement they provide
we might have hope.

Romans 15:4

A PENTECOSTAL APPROACH *to* BIBLE STUDY

WEEK THREE
Through
WEEK ELEVEN

WEEK THREE
THROUGH WEEK ELEVEN

1. From this point on, the group leader will follow the instructional steps as set forth above but apply them to the specific lessons contained in the *Discovery Guide*. It might be fun and informative for the students to think of creative ways to portray what they have learned. For example, some might want to draw or paint a picture of some aspect of James. Others might compose a poem in this regard. The point here is for the students to use different ways of "re-presenting" James to the class. This is also part of the learning process.

2. At the end of *Week Eleven*, the homework assigned for the twelfth week is to reflect on all of the main points that have been learned throughout the course. The students should especially concentrate on the **Devote** and **Discipleship** portions of each lesson and be prepared to share how they have been personally challenged and changed as a result of this study.

A PENTECOSTAL APPROACH to BIBLE STUDY

WEEK TWELVE

The Wrap Up

WEEK TWELVE

This is the wrap-up session where all that has been learned is summarized and presented for discussion by the whole group. In this last session, the group leader should ask questions such as these:

◆ What has God called you to do in light of your study on James?

◆ What might be James' message for the church in general?

◆ How might we **Disciple** others in the challenging but relevant message of James?

A PENTECOSTAL APPROACH *to* BIBLE STUDY

CONCLUDING
THOUGHTS

CONCLUDING THOUGHTS

In one of his final epistles before his martyrdom, Paul exhorts Timothy, "Study to shew thyself approved unto God, a workman that needeth not to be ashamed, rightly dividing the word of truth" (2 Tim. 2:15 KJV). The Greek word for "rightly dividing" is *orthotome* which literally means "to cut a straight line." The image here is of a master craftsman bearing down on a select piece of lumber in order to make an accurate cut. And so it is with the precious Word of God! When we handle the Scriptures, we ought to marshal all of our skills so that we can "cut a straight line" for God and His people. That is, we are to be "expertly incisive" in our interpretations. This can never be a sterile exercise whereby we seek to dominate the Word and bend its message to serve our own ends. After all, the experts in the Law knew where the Messiah was to be born, but they didn't recognize Jesus as their King (Mic. 5:2; Matt. 2:4-6). Rather, "rightly dividing the Word" means to come under its power and to make room in our hearts for God's voice to speak, to call, and to convict. We must first allow the "double-edged sword" of the living Word (Heb. 4:12) to divide us before we can rightly divide the Word. In summary, authentic study of the Bible means to undergo spiritual formation by the Bible. Only after we have been discipled by the Word can we go out and make disciples through the Word. And this is the real goal of IBS: to go out into all the world, making disciples by faithfully teaching the Word of God (Matt. 28:19-20).

Let the message of Christ dwell among you richly

as you teach and admonish one another

with all wisdom through psalms, hymns,

and songs from the Spirit,

singing to God with gratitude

in your hearts.

Colossians 3:16